Visions

of

a new kind

Jayne Aylwin Miller

Visions of a new kind came to me in my dreams and meditations
that only became clear as my life progressed
and as world events developed into the new millennium
Within the effortlessness of poetry I found many answers
and the manner in which they presented themselves
captured the spirit of my questions
until each poem became a perfect gift
that I give to you in the following pages...

Acknowledgments

To the friends who believed in this book enough
to contribute to its manifestation
First edition
All rights reserved.
Copyright ©1987
T and T Publications Limited
P O Box 47095 Trentham
New Zealand

This book may not be reproduced in whole,
part by mimeograph or any other means without permission of

Jayne Aylwin Miller
All rights reserved.
Copyright© 2017
jaynee.com.au

Collage and photo of Uluru by Jayne Miller

Original book cover photo by Julie Callaghan

screenshots from VHS short film
Land of the Warthogs1992

Portrait Photo back cover
Courtesy of Sylvia Storchi
Red Hot Arts
Alice Springs Pride Carnivale 2016

Film strip image: © dule964

*References
http://www.facebook.com/jaynee-96126110660317

With thanks to those people who collaborated to create the film in 1992.
In loving memory of my father and his publishing company for printing the first edition.

Print ISBN: 9780648236900
ebook ISBN: 9780648236917

Catalogue-In-publications (CIP) details available
from the Nation Library of Australia.

Published with the assistance of Publicious Book Publishing
www.publicious.com.au

CONTENTS

I.... Before meeting you....

II.... I am... what I am....

III.... Thoughts.... on life, love, and states of mind....

IV.... Of gender....and identity

V.... New Zealand....

V I.... In the land down under...

VII.... The journey....

VIII.... Mythology and mysticism....

VIII.... Visions....

When the heart is a lonely hunter ....
and skeleton woman arises from the deep
Shed another layer...For lady death is your sister
Who drinks the first,,And last remaining tears of your innocence
So then will you follow the moon
And allow yourself to dance to the tune of empowerment
Losing yourself soul to soul...As you gently bend to kiss the hag
And help her bones unfold
Until finally skin meets skin...Body meets body
Life meets life...Death is transformed
As an everlasting cycle...For the hunter
Within in the journey of love

.... before meeting you ....

Why is it that I feel
we have not yet really met
eye to eye
mouth to mouth.
Is it because you have yet
so much to learn about yourself
and so much traveling to do?
Or is it that you have to
return to the fork in your road
before you started
taking the easy way out,
over the cliff, to avoid the abyss.

Sometimes I feel we are having
our first ever conversations,
and it is our first day
of discovering each other,
when you tell me the history
of your life, and of life itself,
as your soul sees it.

Why has it taken
so long to find your voice?
Where did you lose it?
We have been on a long journey
to find your own unique feeling tone,
as the vehicle of your heart
and the spokesperson of your soul.

We found its sound
in the waters of the stream,
life's most perfect melody,
which contains all sounds
as it silently murmurs over
the rocks sand tells
the most ancient secrets
in its passing.

*You remembered
how you loved the sea
washing through you,
as though you were
a part of its fluidity,
and you felt complete.
So great has been your pain,
so deep has been your longing,
so long has been your loneliness
since then,
even from yourself.*

*And now as the tears
wash the grimace
from the mask
that covers your lovely face,
I see the radiance
come back into your smile.*

*I watch you carefully
from my inner window.
I know you are
as fragile as a leaf
upon the wind.*

*Still curled upon yourself,
the embryonic beginnings of your
self awareness
unfolding bit by bit,
painfully,
and with miraculous effort.*

*As though you are trying
to lift a mountain,
so great are the burdens
you have placed upon yourself.*

And yet all the time,
beside you
also watching you
rediscover yourself,
smiling at the irony
of your confusion,
is your clown.

Like the genie
or the magician
that you wish you were,
he offers you
the magic that you need,
to transform yourself
and emerge from your cocoon.
Maybe when you too
have become a butterfly,
or a moth,
or even as powerful as
a winged spirit of the universe,
you will then find me too
and realize
I was hovering,
waiting for you to emerge
for a long time.
Only then will we
be able to look into the mirror
of each others eyes
and say 'I understand'.

Only then will our
thoughts and feelings
become as one,
complete and timeless,
and we will not need to
speak our minds in words alone.

Only then will our
mouths belong
and we remember where
we met before,
and have no fear of
what may follow
on from there,
and of waiting for too long.

So for now
I'll write your story
and sing your song.
I'll cradle you in my heart
so that nothing can go wrong.
I'll be the nightwatchman
at your temple gate.
I'll tell you who comes back and forth
lest you hear it far too late.
And I wont give up my duty
though I'm weary to the bone.
I wont desert you
while you're waiting
for your spirit to come home.

Poem and Image "Releasing the past: Mothers stories
of their stolen babies: Page 67
Editor : Christine. A. Cole 2008

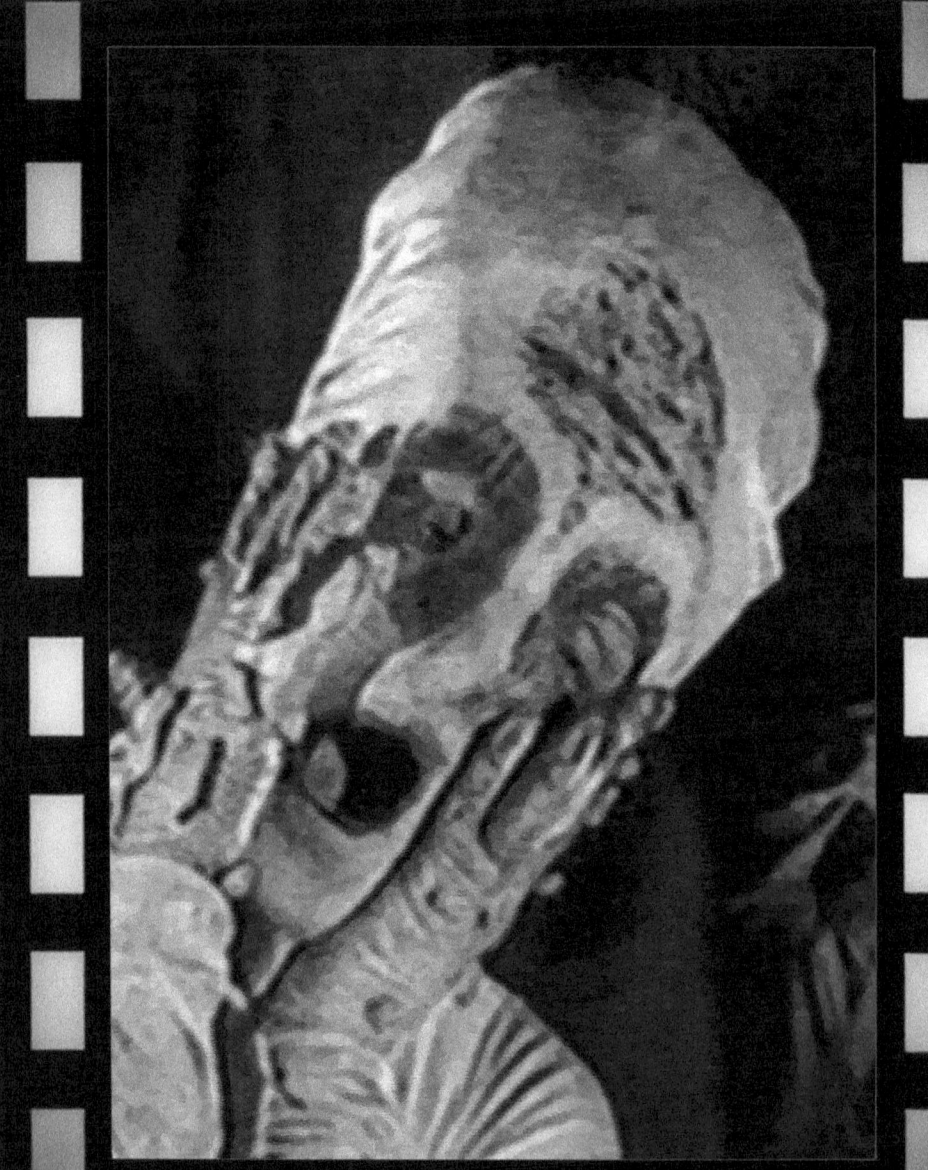

.... I am ....
.... what I am ....

I AM...

Sometimes I wonder
what I'm here for.
I mean
it's got to be a joke.
I mean
maybe I should
laugh
at myself.
That would make
other people
feel better
I think.
Or at least
I might have an excuse
to be myself,
or something,
whatever that is.
Anyway,
I wonder
whether they ever
really wonder
what they're here for.
They look so content
with their illusions.
And I'm too good
at creating
illusions
on top of their
illusions.
What, who, where, why,
therefore art thou,
why not.
...a clown.

WHAT I AM

Mystic clown,
profound,
answers in questions
with no sound.
Expectation don't
frown,
direction lies in,
turn around.
Who's writing symbols
on the ground?
The words absurd
but love profound,
so tell me........
who's the mystic clown?

-down, down
between the minds
find, find
missing links,
body kind,
reminded
rhythm
and of rhyme
beyond time.
So tell me why
mystic clown
I write these symbols
on the ground?

EVOLUTION

In the beginning..It was
as it was in the end,
no trace of the trace-less friend,
world without end.
Nine of them choosing...which one to send.
Hear the message,...comfort the friend.
Leave no trace...of where you've been,
of what you've seen...of the truth,
of the dark and the light
that shall filter through your dreams.
As it was in the beginning
so it shall be in the end.

MEDITATION 2007

It is time for us all ..To pick up our pens
And write the truth..Upon the tablet
Of our hearts

i am i

like the weeping wildflower
in the rain
or the lily and the lotus-flower
that floats on the pond
i am i
that alone
in the stream of life
knowing nothing, knowing it all
searching but not finding other lotus-flowers
thinking i see buds
but most of the time
i see my own reflection
haunted by a shadow
i am i
caught in the 'now'
and struggling to live in timelessness
this is a strange period in history
a spiritual vacuum has begun
people have become mindless, spiritless
inert
world war III depression
and hands grabbing for the last security
money at the expense of friendship
friendship is a dying breed
love has become disillusionment
all peoples secret desires are now obvious
to the discerning eye
how ugly
like slimy creatures
living at the bottom of the pond
they rise to the surface
sea slugs turned inside out
to reveal the horror and futility
of such humankind
what a contrast
what an age of contrast
where are the wildflowers?
there are so few lilies
that rise above the surface
and float on the waters of life
Where are the lotus-flowers?
Where?
Have they all died?

REVOLUTION

Hello soul, here we meet again...
It has been a long time in between meetings...
How much joy and sorrow
and rediscovery of what I already know,
must I go through before I rest forever in this space?
Mountain, tree, moon and sea, reflect my memory upon the air.
all my perfect friends out here.
At home within your warm mystical hold,
because the world of man has left me far too cold.
Humankind I feel such sadness for.
Who can find the garden while they're bricking up the door?
I have no time to linger on the most unnatural human plight,
while I am gratefully cradled in the perfect love of who I am tonight.

MEDITATION 2007

Welcome the rain
like the rhythm of life.
It takes away the pain.
Pain is only the pain of separation
from the flow.
Within the flow there can be no pain.
On the prairie it rarely rains
but when it does
all life runs with it.
The wind in the grass and the animals
they all run with the flow of life again.

MEDITATION 2007

Faeries are the nature spirits of the woods
They are the lights of energy
The vibration and frequency
That most animals can see
Photo from "Jaynee" Facebook Page*(see acknowledgments)

.... thoughts....
of life love and states of mind...

GONE ....NOT FORGOTTEN

Remember the time
Of Leonard Cohen
When we were one
Remember that love
United us then
And even though
Time may pass
Wars may come and go
Human beings may forget but
Love still remains.

LIFE

Oh babe, you wouldn't believe it
if you knew where I'd been.
You wouldn't believe it
if you knew what I'd seen.
Why should you believe it
now that the gypsy is a queen.
I've been in spaces where the faces
are all green.
I've been down in places
where a woman's afraid to scream.
Oh babe, you wouldn't believe it it
if you know what I mean.

DOCUMENTING LIFE

They asked me to write a report on life.
What sweet perfume to the tongues delight,
what bitter taste on the end of my knife.
Sweet memories too long forgotten.
Such fruit within the bowl gone rotten.
All taken for granted, beyond my grasp.
One mans future is another mans past.
One mans truth is another mans lie.
All collected and filed through the reporters eye.....

CREATIVITY...

If art is the science of the soul
in the mirror of creation.
If language is the communion of the mind
and the bridge of the soul.
If music is the language of the emotions
and the food of the soul.
Then drama is the psychological relationship
between all soul, spirit and mind.
And dance is the freedom of the body
to caress the music of the emotions
within the silent language of the human psyche.
What Gods we are when we unify the arts.

LOVE

If our love is real
then somehow it will set us free
and then we can have
our freedom and our love.

If I could be
the bird that whispers in your ear
or the world around you
that wants to give you so much
we would never be parted.

As you grow and change
you become more beautiful
forgive me for being greedy
when I say
I want to stay around.

I wanted to tell you
how I love you
but I got so confused
just like you.
It is funny how it became
distorted
and I became
suspicious of myself
as though I was trying
to tie you down.

If the tragedy of love
is that we forget,
then I'd rather not have
another tragedy this time.
My gift to you
is that I want to remember
and my gift to myself

is that I want you
more than a memory.

When I am addicted
to your love
I try withdrawal
and sometimes
we put each other
through cold turkey.

This feels
like love in cold storage
love in deep freeze
love that once was
but is now not
being returned to me.

I know
you didn't really
like my poetry
when you met me
but you came to understand.
It is a poor excuse
for the experience
but it captures my heart
in my hand
so I can give it to you
again.

In the final hour I
dread the final decision
How can I be expected to choose
between love and love.
This kind of love
is all from the same place
and it chose me,
it seems.

STATES OF MIND

Somewhere in your mind you seek perfection
as though there is a limit to it.

If you don't think you demand much
see if you can fulfill all that you expect others to.

You say you don't want much of what society has to offer,
but as long as there are people around who belong to it
you will always be opened to all of its benefits,
even though you condemn them for its drawbacks.

Your ability to understand amazes me
and your unwillingness to understand stuns me.

All our arguments were, somewhere along the line
initiated by me, while you sat in stony silence
in front of the TV.

Why do people invent a too late, on the time it takes
to figure out what their relationship was worth.
Surely if one has learned something from it
then it was worth it, and it's never too late
to learn something on reflection.

If you could only have understood that my rejection of you
was the degree of my torment over the unresolved past,
then you would have seen the necessity for my resolving it
and not so willingly allowed yourself to get ripped to shreds
trying to stop me.

I am not blaming you for your mistakes
as much as I am annoyed with you
for forgetting to answer your own questions properly,
and distraught that you could even find an excuse
to forget your most important question
in your hour of need.

I want mayonnaise on my tuna sandwich with avocado spread
and heaps of the spice of life to lavish on my bread.
If not for these small luxuries to brighten up my life
I threaten to carve my brain outwith the blunt end of my knife.

TIME

If time is only relative
then you are like a point
on a never ending line.
You see your left as your past,
and your right as your future.
Those ahead of you see you in their past.
Those behind you see you in their future,
and the now is the only thing that is relevant.

MEDITATION 2007

Light a white candle and put it in your left hand
Now place it on the ground to honor the path you have left
And the friends who were on that path
Now let it go
Look to your right hand
Acknowledge this new path with your heart
Now walk in this new direction
Staying centered and balanced

OF LOVE BETWEEN SOULS

Two ancient souls sailed
a highway throughout eternity
and in their passing,
the body recognized,
a desire
and became one -
and now in letting go and being free,
feel my love should you have thirst,
reaching out to you
across the endless spaces in this universe.

MEDITATION 2007

As the tree extends its branches out to life extend your hand
For behind every gesture there is a law and a command of the land
Even in the dark alleys and the rotting garbage,
Even where the machines are designed to carve and cut
The tow trucks the earth moving equipment and the paper pulp mills.

MEDITATION 2007

Home is where the heart is
Where the journey stops
The rest-end
Find peace, like a dove that settles
With an olive branch after a flood
or a drought
or a famine
Be there at the journeys end of life
For always "peace be with you"
Be there with yourself
As you truly are and there you will fnd us too

...Of gender...and identity

GENDER

(a prayer for recognition and equality)
Show us how to cross that bridge
including every gender.
Show us how to build a rainbow
and promise no more tears.
We'd try so hard if we knew how
but we are still blindfolded.
We cannot build a heaven on our own.
We'll have to move together
from our separate sides.
Take it slowly,
painfully aware of losing balance
because we dare,
to cross the once forbidden territory,
for honesty.
Can't help believing the answer
lies somewhere in between.
So show us how to build a rainbow
of oneness and diversity
Show us how to cross that bridge today.

MOTHERHOOD AND LOSS

In the heart of the forest
can you see that gaping hole?
In a pool of broken branches
mud and blood humus and remains
of the unopened bud
that was promised and destroyed in the name of love.
The day of the wounded fox is here again.
Faster and faster, frenzied fear of no escape
from the bloodhound.
Night time blackness, hollow-eyed grief stricken sleep,
waiting for a little more spiritual release.
Why do the things we cannot understand
- cut deep?
Time bound in memory and pain.
Cut the chords of fertility.
Ancient cup lay waste the blame.
God will the adult ever find the child again?
Pray that the sea of these emotions run free and never lose touch with
eternity.
For what I yearn, for what I seek, maybe that of which all poets speak.

SAME LOVE

We met at this time...and touched each others souls
As they lay...within the very heart of creativity
You became yourself...the essence of poetry
And because of your poetic spirit...so did I
We transcended our roles..
And I cried upon the shoulder of my pain...I became joy
I forgave all that I had run from...reunited with my birthright
Reunited by your femininity...into a time of gentleness
Peace and sensitivity...- and it felt good
You and I both...women who trusted
We would never again..
Have to explain the awkwardness and pain of coming out
nor the vulnerability and humiliation of facing society
Because it was our first time...
- And so it was..with gracefulness
As though the universe was watching
Witnessing an act of nature...that confirmed her existence
And united also...in the purity of the moment the air breathed
And probably the moon was smiling...from her hiding place
and kept the secret..

I DON'T NEED YOU

I don't need you to tell me who I am.
I don't need you to understand.
I don't need you to tell me when I'm fat
or when I'm thin.
I don't need you to tell me
where to end or begin.
I don't need you when you turn up late.
I don't need you to break that date.
I don't need you to spend my money.
I don't need you when you're acting funny.
I don't need you to steal my lover.
I don't need you to be my mother.
I don't need you to tell me how to act cool.
I don't need you, you make me look like a fool.
I don't need you to tell me what people don't need.
I don't need you to tell me the world is full of greed.
I don't need the people who won't accept change.
I don't need you, give me back my brains.

POWER GAMES IN REVERSE

Altered ego gotta get away. Buy one more drink and decide to stay
Looking for some trouble, pick the other one up
Looking for a friend and looking for some luck. So
Power games in reverse. The man blows second and the woman blows first
Buy him a beer he has nice hair. He has white teeth and an insolent air oi
Buy him some more drinks and take him to my flat
Grabbing at his power and have him on his back..oi
Power games in reverse...the man blows second and the woman blows first
Four in the morning woken by a smash,
climbing up the drainpipe in my bedroom in my flat..oi
Sometime soon Ill have to pay, one week later in a dangerous way ..oh
Power games in reverse. The man blows second and the woman blows first
Am I that easy am I a white witch?
Am I a stupid female waiting asking for a fix?
Messing up my clothes and dirtying up my bed,
playing my defences and doing in my head ..oi..
Power games in reverse. The man blows second and the woman blows first
Ringing up my girlfriend get me out of here
No one understands what this is all about..oh
Altered ego gotta get away buy one more drink and decide to stay
Power games in reverse. The man blows second and the woman blows first

Audio Music Arrangement "Jaynee" Facebook Page(see acknowledgments)

ON THE EDGE

Caught in the promise...caught in the bind
Peering into each others lives...through half opened blinds
Surrender incomplete
One foot on a new path...self denying the exit
Love running fast...from the precipice.
Feelings block memories pain
They rise and crack the surface again
Is this a blessing or a curse
That one of us should be the first
To love and the first to leave
The last to give and the last to receive
The first to know and the first to deceive the other.
Somewhere down under confusion and mess
Down under fear frustration and stress
Is love still waiting with unopened arms?
Deep as an ocean, mystical calm
How can we love, understand and expand?
What is this woman, what is this man?
Could we return to the garden of Eden?
Would we be safe and our hearts be set free then?
What could be destroyed if we dared to create?
A union of spirit in love for loves sake.

FASHION VICTIMS

I'm a reborn hippie in platform shoes,
Two meter flares and a bald head too
A head full of rings and a body full of shit
An attitude problem hard to shift

Recession clothing is here at last
Gotta get a job while I'm checking out my arse
Check out all the fancy bars and DJ s in town
Good to be the working class and good to see you round.
Saving all my dosh for the big night out
Starving for my body that's what its all about

Fashion victims never die..we just get recycled..trying to survive

Gotta get a hairstyle matching all my clothes
Gotta have the latest gear see me up the road
Well I'm so groovy Ill bring you down
Sorry that you got the flick
Don't mean to muck around

Well I'm so hip with my language too
My friends drive custom-line how about you?
Gotta go to Europe for my holidays
Check out all the labels on my next dole pay
Buy all the hats and the wigs around
Gonna start a hair salon back in town.

Recession clothing is here at last
Recession clothing is here at last
Recession clothing is here at last
Starving for my body that's what its all about
Fashion victims never die
Fashion victims never die

Audio Music Arrangement "Jaynee" Facebook Page(see acknowledgments)

SAME LOVE IN DIFFERENT TIMES

Seventy Four she was under fire..
In eighty four to fight the desire
In ninety four she was idolized here...
Two thousand and four she was normalized yeah

Dark eyed woman..smoke before flame
My hunger your hunger one and the same
Slip down your alley fit my key in your lock
Speak another dialect, what you want is what I got
If I take your fancy and you take my place
Lipstick leather denim and lace

Top bottom in between ..staying on now in the scene
Betty butch is out for the day..cock your fist girl anyway
long hair short hair big boots jeans
high heels hairsprays hormones creams
Dominant passive butch for femme
Change your tactics tell me when

Butch in drag now do your thing..girls that do it on the scene
leave her here on the midnight air ..smokey husky damp with sweat
many more not finished yet
Butch, femme, stone ,bikie ...take charge yeah I do
top bottom baby now..gourmet upfront feel her power
What I want is what I want..what I want is what I choose

Audio Music Arrangement "Jaynee" Facebook Page(see acknowledgments)

...*New Zealand*...

RAINBOW WARRIOR
(Protest song about the bombing of the boat)

Rainbow Warrior beneath the sea,
Rainbow Warrior fighting for me,
Rainbow Warrior just one small boat,
Rainbow Warrior the world can't cope.
Rainbow Warrior they're bombing the sea,
Rainbow Warrior they're bombing me,
Rainbow Warrior while you're afloat,
Rainbow Warrior the world can't cope.
Rainbow Warrior they're setting them free,
An atoll in paradise is where they'll be.
A ten year sentence reduced to three,
As we all bow our heads for humanity.
Rainbow Warrior the name of peace,
tears in my bread because I have to eat,
Rainbow Warrior begging them please,
For a rainbow now and a nuclear freeze.

Audio Music Arrangement "Jaynee" Facebook Page(see acknowledgments)

AFTERSHOCK

After all it has been
As long as the days go by
For sure to be true Ill try
With you in my heart
Still I long to be free to fly into the sky

Then again beyond this wilderness
Where chained to my pain
I swear upon this cross
I cannot say goodbye
When some have lived and
Some have died
I just cant say goodbye

So it seems that it can never be
before us or behind us yet in between,
In between we dream and we try and maybe
We fly into a new life for a day it seems
The butterfly has wings

(after the 2011 Christchurch Earthquake)
Aftershock Documentary Theme Song "Jaynee" Facebook Page*(see acknowledgments)

WORLD PRAYER FOR OUR CHILDREN'S FUTURE

And shall the lion lie down with the lamb
If not the living shall envy the dead
Is there a choice between the quick and the dead
Do you think we could live peacefully instead.
"Nations playing with fire, will you burn up
In the fires of your own creation
Will you be forever responsible
For this hell on earth".
Oh my children!

So shall the lion lie down with the lamb
And could the living walk free on the land
Do you think there is a future ahead
Do you think we could live peacefully instead.

Audio Music Arrangement "Jaynee" Facebook Page(see acknowledgments)

STOCKS AND SHARES...

I think I'll go out and cut my hair
I want to buy some stocks and shares
Get out a mortgage on my wife
I want to pay debts for the rest of my life.
I think I'll quit my youthful dreams
Support multi-nationals latest schemes
Sell all my stocks while the dollar is high
Impress all my friends with the cars I can buy.
I want to be rich I don't want to be broke
Tell all my friends that I'm a good bloke
I don't like my pay check or government tax
I won't join the dole queue if .. shares wax.

STOCKS going up and SHARES going down
STOCKS and SHARES are hitting the ground
STOCKS are climbing and I wonder why
More STOCKS and SHARES have reached for the sky.

(substitute stocks n shares for current company names)
*Audio Music Arrangement "Jaynee" Facebook Page(see acknowledgments)

WHAT IS HAPPENING TO MY COUNTRY

When I was young I loved those songs
About future humankind.
I used to live a vision of the world as one.
I used to heed their promises and warnings often sung.
But I never thought I'd see the future past.
I never thought I'd see the damage done.
It was just the ultimate in disappointment with time.
There was a time when I became outcast
When from my friends and family I'd part
As though the year of twenty five had come
As though the curse of Armageddon had won
And though to my own self I could not be true
The pain of being a woman of heart who knew.
It was just the ultimate in disappointment with lies.
And now I see I am misunderstood
And now I see most people are not good
And now I see I will not change their lies
And now I see I cannot pay their price
And now I see people confused and lost
And now I see their loneliness and what it cost.
It is just the ultimate disappointment in humankind.

MUD CRAB

With slow deliberate wisdom eyes first-
a glimmer in the dark shadow of the hiding place
or was it your imagination?
no- but watch very carefully
you will become sure- the eyes are watching you
even when you can't see them.
Then like magic something moves, the stone has life.
No! As it changes shape, from underneath- the crab,
still eyes fixed purposeful intent
self-conscious and aware after all
the environment is privileged to have crabs there.
So you look at each other from this safe distance,
the separation of water and land,
and in her hesitation you feel perplexed at first
waiting for her to scuttle back beneath the rock
which is not yet too far away.
But slowly you learn the language
of subtle movements, and long pauses
which you are tempted to interrupt.
But caution you've realized, she feels your mood and possible intent
any restlessness would be a step too soon,
sending her further into one of her many hiding places
and somehow you don't want that
Not yet- while this quiet miracle of contact exists,
while you feel her presence- a privilege so rare.
Then all at once she reads your mind
or is it just the change of tide,
when suddenly
she's gone.

....in the land down under....

THE HEART OF ULURU

There is a dark heart
in the white history of Uluru
That belongs to the USA
There is a light heart
In the dark history of Uluru
That belongs to a timeless tradition
There is a red heart
In the center of Australia
that bleeds and cries
There is a cancer in the landscape
Called Pine Gap
That needs to be removed.
Australia as a people
May we break away
From the tyranny and control
Of the ones we call US of A
May the guardians of the dream-time
Come back to life out here once more
So that the healing can begin

Photo and poem*"Jaynee" Facebook Page*(see acknowledgments)

AUSTRALIAN WALKABOUT NATION

Walkabout Nation came to roost
Upon a barren landscape of hidden truth
Clothed in the contradictions
Of cultural diversity
Australia sprang from a black mans landscape
In an unknown universe.
So we are crossing song lines and weaving maps
Talking our stories to fill in the gaps
Blending races and healing souls
Retracing our bloodlines to fill in the holes

What does it take to create a great nation
A flag or a banner, some artists creation?
Or the mindful awareness of words lesser known
That address a true future on the walkabout home

CANT SEE THE TREES FOR THE COAL SEAM GAS

I don't want to sing no protest songs
Too many protests too much wrong
Australia raped by coal seam gas
The last land grab to pay no tax

Cant see the forest for the trees
Cant see the trees for the C.S.G.
Great Aussie swindle of the century

Evaporation process ponds
They all leak and they are all wrong
Bully up our neighbors frack up our land
Leave our country with the cash in their hands

We walked the streets to stop the mining
The mainstream media was not behind us
We locked up our gates in our neighborhoods
But the government approved them to frack in our woods

Because they cant see the forest for the trees
They cant see the trees for the C.S.G.
Greatest Aussie swindle of the century

(The latest C.S.G. rush to harness fossil fuel instead of renewable energy)
LIVE Music Video Performance Jaynee Facebook Page(see acknowledgments)

BALGOWLAH HUTS
(early settler fisherman's huts Sydney North Shore
... artist squats until mid 1980s)

We are the hut dwellers of Crater Valley.
We are not a fantasy
but a lot of people
ignore us or deplore us
having sanctuary.

We don't mind spending our time
without fluoride in our water.
The wind, the sun and sea
are our luxuries.
Laughing at the ferries and the neon lights,
wedding cakes and sideshows all with slot machines alike,
this pantomime of Sydney harbor late at night.

These huts were built by fisherman Pearce
in 1920 on this land,
who began this small tradition with his hands.
He built these walls from rocks and driftwood,
and housed his family in the depression.
It was the property of the army
until they sold the land
and kept the huts hidden
under National Park protection.

Now they want to pass a law,
that when the last hut falls
they exist no more.
Our species are small
but no less antique
than old Sydney-town
of which they all speak.

These huts are our backbone,
our family tree.
Where else can the old
still exist with the new,
where the skinks and the water dragons
look at you.
Once in this bush lived an old time community
deep in the heart of the twentieth century.

SYLVIA AND THE DINGO
(Alice Springs NT)

Sylvia and the dingo went walking in the park
The sun was on the juniper, the sky had gone quite dark

There was a ghostly silence that night brings to the air
With images of peoples lives emerging not quite there

As if by random stroke of luck that they should be together
Strangers from another time and known each other forever

Way back in Alice Springs where the desert center glows
They said "hello" on the river Todd where the water rarely flows

The dingo howled and wagged his tail attracting her attention
Then ran away before she could play at human intervention

But then returned to say goodbye one rugged winters morn
By turning for a backward glance on his search for food forlorn

Come follow me he seemed to say but then he knew she wouldn't
For even though she wanted to play I think he knew she couldn't

SYDNEY'S RED LIGHT DISTRICT

Well late last night he came into the Piccolo Bar
and he came and went to the call of the moon
Until a voice said 'from whence shall ye all abstain',
but what would you do if the call of the moon called for you?
To me and you it all remained the same,
to use no willpower and yet abstain

Come out of the darkness come out of the cold
the earth grows old people sell their souls.
Preacher gives you a reason not to plot such treason
and waste your time with foolish desires
with promises and lies tempting stones to bread
and setting your veins on fire.
you know you still have a heart of gold,
but you're twisting it into metal collecting rust and mold.

COMMUTING IN SYDNEY

Dead pan faces uplifted eyes
Cardboard cabbages passing by

Derelict at the roadside
Trying out his act
Hurls abuse with no excuse
At his victims back
Staggers to the bus stop
Sees a lovely piece
Tells her where to take her charms
And stick it up with grease.

Dead pan faces uplifted eyes
Cardboard cabbages passing by.

He spies perchance a loaded bus
Waiting at the lights
He's full of gin and dirty flirt
Waiting for a fight
Bawls his bit with some great gusto
Across the street through the open window

Dead pan faces uplifted eyes
Cardboard cabbages passing by.

Bus stops off to drop its lot
Here comes one classic punk-rock
Strawberry feathers for his hair
Safety pins hang everywhere
Careful posing his electric guitar
"Watch out boys" this one will go far
Walk down the aisle clanking tin
Leather gear salvaged from some rubbish bin.

Dead pan faces uplifted eyes
Cardboard cabbages passing by.

A passing pedestrian..in front of the old bus
Takes five steps forward..and two back thus
Taking twice as long to cross the busy street
While he strides now forwards.. now retracing his feet.

Dead pan faces uplifted eyes...cardboard cabbages are passing by.

GRAFTON'S NIMBY BRIDGE

Our bridge is as bent as a dogs hind leg
once it was a train track way back when
They put a dredge to the water laid the brick steel and mortar
in the heat of the day..in the heat of the day..
Well that old bridge shes falling down
bit by bit and all around
With traffic stalling creeping and a crawling
we pray to reach the other side
..The other side... the other side
Well its fifty years on and were still praying
from our grandfathers time to the new generation
We just cant decide on the second bi pass
because we don't want the bridge in our backyard
The second bridge is like the second coming
we have prayed for the new one that damn hard
We want a new bridge and we want it today
but don't let the old one slip away
And don't put the bridge in our backyard

Well every new election *R.M.S. plan erection
of a brand new bridge in the fiftieth selection
They plan to dredge the water lay the brick steel and mortar
in the heat of the day...in the heat of the day...

Dedicated to RM.S (Roads and Maritime Services)
New bridge in old Grafton New South Wales
LIVE Music Video Performance Jaynee Facebook Page*(see acknowledgments)

SHOE SHINER

Stayed too long
In this city
Trying to make a break.
Seen a lot of changes
More buskers on the street.
False promise of a future
Delaying your defeat.

No talent in the nightclubs
No rhythm in the beat
Just another female singer
Who cant get off her seat.
You know
You can't shine the shoes
Off a rich man's feet.

But I've got a song
I've got something to say.
So you go your way
And I'll stay.
I've got a dream
To sing about places
And people I've seen,
And it's too late now
To change my life
And go away.
I can't go back and live like that anyway.

No talent in the nightclubs
No rhythm in the beat
Just another female singer
Who can't get off her seat.
You know
You can't shine the shoes
Off a rich mans feet.

MIDSUMMER NIGHT'S DREAM

It was the time of the
"Flowers and the Dream"
It was the beginning of your life purpose
and i the mad poet with the scheme

i saw my face in your face
i felt my love and your love
in your silent primeval scream
and in the collective unconscious of this time
came an omen for you and for me

and shall i write a poem for you
about a pure white flower
and an impossible dream

i shall write a song for you and then
as you smile and nod
I'll know you understood
the magic

it seems the circumstances had woven
all the pieces into one
and there we were
two angels
and yet two human beings

maybe it has been done before
maybe a well known theme
but you were my guardian angel
and i was your long lost dream

–

*dedication to Lindsay Kemp and Michael Matou
who influenced my first Music Video Performance
"Land of the Warthogs"
Jaynee Facebook Page*(see acknowledgments)

.... the journey ....

POSSIBLE EXPLANATION OF THE GAME

PLAYERS.....

ntelligent people become rogues and vagabonds and robin hoods as they see life is a game
but...
Wise intelligent people realize that it is a deadly serious game, rather like russian roulette, and learn to play their game of not playing games, while they're playing....
Enlightened wise intelligent people only pretend they're playing a game of not playing games while they're playing, because they have the powerful vision to see the game before it starts, and can stop it where they will.
They have the true power and control.

RULES

One does not have to be ultimately good to be on the chessboard.
One only has to have: - an opponent to learn from
- know a lot of different rules,
and have a subtly disguised set of rules for oneself.

PARADOX OF THE CRIMINAL AND THE SAINT
(how not to avoid a nuclear holocaust at zero hour)

"Dumb" is
when you realised
you allowed something to happen,
that you could have stopped happening,
because you knew all the facts,
even though everyone else
thought you were mad, or at least exaggerating.
And you watched while it happened,
allowed it with your idealistic notion
that everyone has the right to their own decisions
and that you must be wrong,
by the law of averages, how could so few people
be right?

And so you thought you were dumb
when actually you were smart.
You abdicated responsibility.
There was so little time to reflect
before the button was pushed.
And so the wrong decision, the wrong action was started.
The snowball started rolling,
with the potential of gathering all you and your
friends in its path.

Like your best friend pressed the button
while you were standing there to stop him,
and all because you didn't believe in yourself.
So you condemned the innocent as well as the ignorant.
"Is that dumb!"

So now you had to act dumb,
and tell no one what was happening,

saving yourself only to watch the torture,
or join the snowball like a true martyr,
watching your best friend shoot himself in the head
with his self-righteous ignorance.
And your karma was
to know you could have stopped it.

But he wont listen now.
You let him be right.
And so you wait and pray
the destruction wont begin,
and he prays it will.
And your best friend is your worst enemy.
And you pray
you wont have to see it.
You pray you wont have to pick up the broken
dead bodies with your broken dead heart,
and you wouldn't even have the right
to say- I told you so!

Like the opponent who had his delicate life
in your clumsy thick hands.
In true irony- all you could say was.....

It happened too fast.
I didn't have time to consolidate
the wisdom of my past mistakes.
The time came to act without time,
like the criminal he chose to judge,
and knighthood he believed he would gain.
Four quartered,
martyred,
moral disgrace,
the saint became the criminal,
and the criminal the saint.

SOBRIETY

Vain imagining
and reality,
mixed up my dream
till I could see,
what I thought
I wanted to be,
letting me hide
from the pain
and separation inside,
from feeling the dead
and the empty.

They led me false prophets,
to want paradise,
too much to then see
the warning lights that bled,
in the raw confusion
of this forsaken head.

Veiled in smokescreens and the like,
employed like cushion buffers,
should the dreaded flash,
insight,
scatter illusion and reveal,
the sordid truth
in broad daylight,
rebellious dreams of self ideal,
youth hellbent for self destruction.

Taken trips for loss of reason,
conned by every scene there is,
in search of a new identity.
They saw me there,
when all the time

I thought they saw me here.
Till in the end
I realized,
that only I had been the one,
who had not seen
through my disguise.

So I lay
exposed
for all to see,
human weakness
lunging vultures slough and bleed,
to death- the realness of this state,
themselves have lost, in all their
sneering, and self needing hate,
while I allowed them to participate
such sordid witchcraft!

Till quickly said,
no more these bones their beauty shed,
no more to lie upon a bed,
of such impending doom.
And raised these eyes, so long dust covered
in self disgust to then discover,
my lost horizon in the blue,
and I began to journey to
on looking back
- in recompense
Thank Christ the end
of ignorance!

ANGER

Tune in, let go
It's you
Crying to be recognized
It's you
Trying to survive.

Big bloke indifference
Wont tell you where you stand
Who's friend and lover sits the fence
And offers you a hand.

Create some more excuses
Like everybody else
Are you going to work it out
Good friends stick together
They say that's where it's at
Yeah good friends don't get angry
Keep pretending to be nice.

Abstinence is a cop out
Don't want that 'state' no more
Why hang about
Like no one cries
Who hasn't been to war
Shake off the guilt or
Are you going to let them
Make a wanker of you too
Until you feel the anger
Grow inside of you.

Feel the power in letting go
Love and anger
Feel the same
In your pulse
You are aware
You trust your body
With your mind
And moved them demons
From behind.

Not hard you perceive
Body reveals
What mind receives
And self stops fooling itself
Negativity gives you a rest
While guilt has a habit of pushing up
All those demons you've got in your head
Pretending to be the shakes
Paranoia, the blues
Till you feel you're going insane
You're so confused.

I don't want your body
You can keep your soul
I don't want to tell you
What to do
But are you scared to drop that mask?
Do you think your friends
Will stand and laugh?
Do you think you'll uncover
Some terrible truth?
And well- what is the point
In becoming aware?
Like an empty head on borrowed time?
You don't believe in being fair on yourself
Blame your kin who first took your pride
And lovers who hide their true feelings inside
And all because ..life is so uncivilized.

WALKING THROUGH THE WALL

Stuck on a rung of the internal ladder
left standing before the invisible wall
frozen within this inner landscape
remembering the greatest riddle of all.

'The one who knows everything
knows nothing at all
the one who knows nothing
knows it all- talking to the wall'

Recalling the walls we have cursed as we met them
'Where the riddle's in the answer,
and the answer's a question'
Banging our heads till the blood runs red hot
in the battle of no battle against paradox.
Breathing becomes shallow, skin becomes cold,
feeling fear and confusion as the puzzle unfolds.
Till the mind becomes blank and the flesh becomes weak,
until only the rhythms of breathing can speak.

Then mysteriously into the blank screen of our minds
projects an image with a question it wants us to find.
Our self doubt says 'that's crazy', but we have to pursue
for the truths in ourselves and the image a clue.

We regress to a time when we last felt completed
and recall all the riddles of self doubt we defeated.
We remember in shock the flip side of self doubt
was belief in ourselves that we never let out.

With great pain as we ponder the time it has taken
to come back to the land where our souls were forsaken.
Till we can speak to our teacher
we can watch the bricks fall,
then without hesitation we can
walk through the wall.

Audio Music Arrangement "Jaynee" Facebook Page*(see acknowledgments)

DEPARTED

A child of the twilight world
heard the piper's tune.
One of the chosen few
to hearken to the call
so soon
the twilight and the dusk will fall
on all of us.
May we not question
insincerity
but in serenity
herald this day.
She cries to all of us
to let her life be,
because like clowns
we search for answers
we've already found.
We ride a merry-go-round
and do not see,
and do not feel our feet upon the ground.

And now,
is this child of the brave new world
returning to her throne?
Crying to a dying world
to leave such fights alone.
We will not find our answers
in tomorrow,
but today.
So much is yet to be made known
the work of those who stay.
Understanding comes within
this sacred moment
of time we're in,
and only we
can throw that time away.

THE MISSING MIRROR

Looking for yourself
you run to find completion
in human life a reason to aspire,
yourself admire.
You seek to teach them
your soul to reach them,
divided only feeling your desire,
while they find their missing mirror
in your eyes.

And you desire, require- release from your own burden
and die to find a thousand deaths
were born before completion
where you find the missing mirror in your eyes.

The smell of death is putrid,
mind too weak to compromise,
to keep alive false hope
your body will not hypnotize.
Rejection, expectation tried to humanize,
reveals your broken heart
under a microscope- and in
the lines between your epitaph
you wrote,

How you desire, require- release from your own burden,
and die to find a thousand deaths
were born before completion
where you find the missing mirror in your eyes.

Such words should future humankind recognize
all that your depression did not paralyze,
that pray you not forever bewail this earthling's plight
in returning to the garden of your soul tonight,
in the footsteps of the ancient of the old,
the missing mirror to your eyes, your eyes, unfold.

THE GIFT

Why don't these people understand
that my love and life
are lying in my hands.
I cannot sell my words and deeds
for such a low price.
I speak of real people and events
I paint a poem of life.
I still believe
there is a direction for humanity.
It does not lie in compromise and lies,
or stealing one human life force
because yours dies.
When will people understand
true knowledge is so precious,
tread carefully tread fearfully,
otherwise rich people with hearts like beggars,
will trample you with their desires.

BAMBOO ENERGY

I stood within the bamboo leaves
at twilight
and realized what
only our moments of self doubt
can take away.
I touched white leaves
against a darkening blue sky
protection.
I stood encircled upon
this sacred altar
and paid homage
to the crickets
who called me here.
I bowed to my knees
in gratitude
and promised to return.
My skin glowed white
with bamboo energy and
healed my sadness.

.... *mythology and mysticism* ....

LOST CIVILIZATION
(Dream 1984)

In the mighty room she stands,
epitomize an empire doomed.
Living legend, woman of state
loss of pride, hiding inside
a mummified hieroglyph.
This sacrifice upon her head,
curse of Egypt's, living dead,
threatened men whose deeds and lies
will haunt her soul for many lives.
Wander in the stately tomb,
in dread to see behind that room.
Hope destroyed, the self destruction
of sovereign to empty shell,
a man who once all power held.
The room with windows on all sides,
reveals lost empire once the pride,
that angry mans dominion.
Worth plundered now to empty vanity,
pyramid to human insanity

THE FALL OF DIVAK
(Divak- our wrong choices and the Sphinx - our inner truth)

What self destruction does he reap?
He hangs himself because he tries to hang the Sphinx.
He does not rise to paradise, but sinks beneath,
into the world of good and evil and here he creeps.
And here he tries to hide from his higher spirit
that he tries to kill inside.
He will not solve the riddle until he relinquishes false pride.
He tries to burn his bridle.. he tries to burn his reins.
He doesn't know how to remove them .he's struggling and strangling in pain.
He's ripping the flesh off the prisoners and sticking them up his veins.
Now the bond and the Sphinx will leave him.
He will not understand why they came.
For his fear of the power within them
has made him deny them again.
The Sphinx will sing songs at his grave-side,
return him his burden of shame.
He has made of himself a false martyr
and his life ends in empty games.
He has squandered the last of his energy
and burns himself up in his flames.
Now only the phoenix can save him,
and restore him back to his own name.

STORY OF THE MOON AND THE SUN
(A tribute to the indigenous legends of all native people)

The moon longed for a chance to reunite with the sun.
She had so long been made to cast long shadows
throughout the earth, and in her loneliness torn apart,
till scarcely a glimmer of hope remained.
Yearning still for her lost lover, hardly daring to breathe
in case one day her lover would come again.
Did you notice? - never mind!
The moon, she knew about the darkness and of changes to our souls,
of lust and hidden wantonness snake pits and open holes.
She longed to find one ray of hope, instead she found reflection.
Her crying was her dying breath, "Oh sky, give us redemption!"
It seemed you died at sunset you never saw her light.
It seemed you ran away before the ending of the night.
Could she eclipse your splendor for one second of your life?
You gave love with your left hand, and you took it with your right.
Did you notice? - never mind!
Now she travels her lonely path of destiny again.
The sun stayed far too briefly he may as well have never come.
It is her beauty that is born of love lost pain.
She lives to tell the story again and yet again.
He was only playing, changing all her moods for fun.
And so continues the saddest story of the moon and of the sun.

LOST FAITH

So maybe I believed in magic
and made sacrifices upon the altar of that belief,
and now my world has been disintegrated.
Now that the magician
has left the apprentice
I feel betrayed.
It was not your fault.

It was simply that you lost your need for flying carpets
in the hour of my graduation,
and the gift became separated
from the power,
the innocence of the child
and the crushed flower.

Now I cannot stand the vacuum,
left in space,
dangling in a black hole,
hanged by the rope I once walked,
branded the fool by my failure.

And you expect me to accept the change,
the bitter resolution
of all you have forgotten.

Forgive me as I compromise
and ignore the warnings
about the comfort of a pathway
that can only lead me under.
Forgive me as I trade my ideals
for a temporary shelter.

I have also paid for my selfishness,
in the mirror of fear and lost hope,
and it is nothing new to be slain by the hands
that once loved me,
punished for my self indulgence,
love caved in upon itself.

PIPE DREAMS

All those people
who have put you down
who laugh at what they call
your pipe dreams,
show them whose really
made of steel,
show them fake from real,
trust yourself and you will
know how to live.
Show them how to feel,
because they can't see beyond
what they think is here and now,
because they don't know
there is no time, no hour,
it's all in how you let yourself
that creates now.
And if I find the secret to success,
I can't give you any formula,
you must find your own recipe
you must set your own dreams free,
till your dreams are real

MATHEMATICAL COSMOLOGY

Magic numbers..,mystic wonders,
Reflection, projection ,of a scientific age.
Scientific preparation for the universal day.
Superstition, suspicion investigate omission
and light the way. evolution, progression,
spiritual regression, man's incomprehension
of the laws that he obeys.
Thought history was turning,
when in truth it was transforming,
magician manifested to the calling of the day.
Energy and yearning, inspiration learning,
transmutation, balance, ended paradox this way.
And those from the future call to you through timeless time,
saying the way of the future to heaven has come.
Time to turn our numbers back
to timelessness and one.

PARADISE LOST

Listen to the calling of the wind inside your soul.
Be still enough to let true love unfold.
Believe your dreams they are the messengers you seek,
while men of forked tongue steal in promises
they ask us all to keep.
Like the ancient mariner and the albatross,
the pied piper and the cripple lost,
returning with the burden of a message heard too late,
bearing a cross and crying "Had you heard?
Eternity came and left on the wings of a bird.
We think the albatross"
And all this time
the fish was swimming still both ways,
preparing for primeval gasp of air,
and turning fell straight down a waterfall,
to find rebirth inside the largest lotus flower of all,
then turning into eagle and to albatross
rejoined with the children of this paradise lost.

MEDITATION 2007

We are sitting in the tall grass smoking the pipe
and remembering how
before aeroplanes there was a very different understanding of flight
We used to fly with the spirit of the eagle.
Nowadays people fly in aeroplanes.
Human beings need to remembered how to fly like the eagle
Meanwhile we are sitting in the tall grass
smoking the pipe
to celebrate the remembering

.... visions ....

VISION OF THE LAND OF THE WARTHOGS
(Dream 1984)

I started out in the Land of Plenty.
Where the sun was still shining,
and the children were one,
and their thoughts knew no evil,
their days were not numbered,
and the colors were brilliant,
where the prophets would come,
and their love knew no limit
for the promise of one.

But on turning around, I escaped from the circle,
and on looking behind a dirty old shed,
I wondered what magic lay in the dark colors,
when I fell to the ground, to the Land of the Dead.
Where the earth was all flat and the cold mud was boiling,
in the Land of the Warthogs I found my head.

"Aah but I am not a Warthog" - I said.

And an old man came and stood by the pools,
and he held my hands
and he said, "We are the Damned".
"Aah- I have warts upon my hands!"

Why did I look beneath the earth?
Flying- we are flying,
don't go, don't go away.
Wait- wait,
someway back, someway back
to the Land of the Plenty.
And I discovered,
I discovered a crystal clear stream,
so clear was the water, that I could not see it.

Banished! don't go- Banished don't go!
We've been banished, we've been banished
from the Land of the Plenty!
No! - I am not one of you.
I will not be damned!
And a voice said-

"Cleanse thyself from the Land of the Warthogs
that you may join your family in the blinding light
of the uplifted Generation"

And I discovered, in that water,
in that crystal clear water,
that I was being transformed,
transformed back,
into one of the Land of the Plenty,
and my colors changed.
Flying, -don't go away I'm coming back!

And so

I returned to the Land of the Plenty,
the sun is still shining,
the children are one,
their thoughts know no evil,
their days are not numbered,
the colors are brilliant
where the prophets will come,
and their love knows no limit
for the Promised One.

*dedication to Lindsay Kemp and Michael Matou
who influenced my first Poetry Video Performance
"Land of the Warthogs"
LIVE Poetry Video Performance "Jaynee" Facebook Page*(see
acknowledgments)

RETURN OF THE ICE AGE...

Electra-magnetic shifts between the earth and the moon,
solar flares from the sun,
molten lava on the earth's crust
in times to come.
Melting polar ice caps,
shifting axis moving all the land mass,
creations purging crisis,
and all our evolution come to this!!!

Did the ones before the ones we call the human race
destroy all evidence of their existence before our human state
Did the lucky ones escape?
Aliens to us , forever UFO's out there,
and humanity return again to the equivalent of the ape?

INFORMATION WARS

Dear Spirit..my hand drags across the page
In final exhaustion my blood turns white
My heart is almost leaden now..knowing the lies that have yet
to creep into the hearts and minds of people in these troubled times
Where no earthly spirit is pure enough to guide us
No heart clean and undefined
The clouds are muddy with the pollution of the earth
God grant that I don't see the last drop of rain dry up
God grant that my own people do not lock me up
Through their misunderstanding of my tears

FOR AFRICA

(Dream 1992)

I will lift up mine eyes ..and turn them to the west
From whence shall come my release
I have seen thy great famines Johannesburg
In the country of my birth that zaps my strength

Audio Music Arrangement "Jaynee" Facebook Page*(see acknowledgments)

MEDITATION 2009

"Abide with me and thee"
As thee with me
holy three forever young
Among the recent events and old traditions
Molehills and snake skins of the past millennium
Believe in me to see you throughout these times
These times are greater than anguish alone
For much changes in the passing of an emperor
For it is the last stand, the bastion of these ones
We call the tyrants.. I will not forsake thee"

NIGHTMARES OF THE ELITE
(Dream 1986)

I see the working class
and the middle class moron
from my wooden tower.
I am not safe anymore.
They are coming in my windows.
They are breaking through my door.
Two stories up without a ladder.
How did they get in there?
They must have supernatural powers.
They want to kill my spirit.
They want to suck me off the floor.
How can I keep them away?
I'll have to pray, I'll have to pray.
There's more of them walking out of the sea.
They are not real, they will not let me be.
Their skin is of gangrene
but their clothes are clean.
With a ghostly deadly aura,
they haunt me in my dreams.

WHERE ANGELS TREAD

Owe no one nothing and leave nothing behind you babe,
nothing to bind you to your past.
Go where they can't find you,
if you want to keep moving, where they can't blind you from your path.

True intent is unbent, heartfelt worship,
heaven sent, destination well spent,
inspiration leads where
only angels dare to tread.

Pay your own way..collect the debts
that are owed to you everyday.
Don't ask a person for anything
they won't give away.
They weave a tangled web and life delays,
until you trick yourself and stay,
until you think you can't live any other way.

True intent is unbent, heartfelt worship,
heaven sent, destination well spent,
inspiration leads
where only angels ever went.

TWILIGHT ZONE

Gods of our ancestors call upon us now.
Pan is in the trees playing his flute.
The sorcerer became a sorcerer from pain.
The time is now, so soon, and yet so long,
We waited until the sun sank
Below the horizon,
And seagulls floated upon the waves
Of silent music
Above the waters of time.
Encased within these mortal bodies,
We danced within our souls, like dying.
Caught between the twilight zones,
Saluting to the sun, and crying out
"Great Holy Oneness"
"Why has humankind forsaken us?"

VISION OF THE REFUGEE CRISIS
(Dream 1989)

In a dream I saw a future promised mountain.
All that the giants of wood stock had so far planned.
I saw their children trying to create a brave new world,
turning with one eye on their cities made of sand.

Some were singing gypsies, in a dedicated festival to humans.
Makeshift shelters, homage to a future refuge,
rejoicing in the freedom of their calloused hands.
United in the wake of their original songs.

Until a thief from the twilight world
came and scattered all their cities into dust.
It was the seal of an ancient tradition
of gravestones and blood.
The outcast demon left his shadow in the valley,
and out of the confusion of lost purposes,
came a black horse of greed and lust.

While those that were innocent
were lifted by their only alternative,
and with the eye of a snake determined the shadows
became blobs that had names.
"Oh prolific source of music,
begin once more to flow within our veins,
only the power of the music
can heal our grief and shame,
oh deadly flame".

And at the end of the dream,
I was left with one question.
Why should it be so that most people are dead?
For it seemed that the gypsies were the only survivors,
as they packed their supplies
and they quietly fled,
turned their backs on their past,
left their caravan sheds.
Weary limbs walk the deserts,
one more chance in their blood,
now all that is left
is their tracks in the mud.

THE PROMISE
(Dream 1992)

even as the hair from my face
became a blackened match
i held it to my eyes
and the flame of life
reappeared at its tip

and as i held it to the light
it became as brilliant
as the sun of reality
where-upon
i was turned by some unseen force
to face an ancient oriental man
who said

"this is the beginning of the end
this is the war to end wars
this is the time when humankind
will achieve their greatest point
of spiritual maturity
and the true birth of the new millennium
will have
begun"

so indeed beneath me
i saw a huge city rise
at a right angle to my dimension
and on refocusing my vision
i saw it emerged from
a hole in the ground
from where it had been hidden so long

i watched this ancient secret
spring to life in one second
with all its twenty first century technology
and i was outside of earth time
joyous at our planets excellent balance
of spirit mind and matter
reunited.

MEDITATION 2007

END OF THE WAR ON TERROR

This war on terror
People have forgotten joy
We record some events
And others are not recorded
Eventually this war will be over
And the truth will be known
In the meantime
Eat well
Be happy
And stay close to nature

www.ingramcontent.com/pod-product-compliance
Lightning Source LLC
LaVergne TN
LVHW051507070426
835507LV00022B/2968